JAPANESE *kimono* DESIGNS

SHÔJIRÔ NOMURA
TSUTOMU EMA

DOVER PUBLICATIONS, INC.
MINEOLA, NEW YORK

Bibliographical Note

This Dover edition, first published in 2006, is a new selection of designs from two rare Japanese portfolios published in 1931 and 1932. A new note has been written specially for this edition.

DOVER *Pictorial Archive* SERIES

International Standard Book Number: 0-486-44426-0

Manufactured in the United States of America
Dover Publications, Inc., 31 East 2nd Street, Mineola, N.Y. 11501

着物

JAPANESE KIMONO DESIGNS

L ITERALLY the Japanese word for "thing to wear," the term "kimono" has come to refer specifically to the straight-cut robe that is the Asian garment most familiar to the people of the west. The kimono has a long ancestry that can be traced back to China. By the eighth century, Chinese-style robes were being worn by the Japanese court. In the tenth century, during the Heian period [794–1192], Japanese culture began to move away from Chinese traditions and to develop its own sensibility. The Heian period was one of elegance and refinement, and great emphasis was placed on dress. The basic garment for court women was square cut, but was much more voluminous than the modern kimono. As many as twelve different layers might be worn, each slightly larger in size than the last and a slightly different color. The innermost layer, the *kosode* (literally "small sleeve," so named for its narrow arm openings), was the forerunner of the modern kimono. The Kamakura period [1192–1333] that followed was a period of turmoil and warfare, and the elegance of the Heian court gave way to simpler styles. By the late fourteenth century, the humble kosode took center stage as an outer garment, and by the mid-fifteenth century was worn by men and women of all classes.

Despite variations in size, material, decoration, and number of layers worn at a time, the kimono has remained a square-cut body with square-cut sleeves. In this, it differs dramatically from western dress, which tends to follow the lines of the body. This deemphasis on the shape of the wearer shifts the focal point of the garment from line to surface, and the kimono's unbroken rectangular sections make it a perfect canvas for the decorative arts. The demarcation between art and craft, so clear in the West, is non-existent in Japan and an article of clothing is as worthy of artistic endeavor as a painting. Many well-known artists in other fields designed kimonos and other textiles as well.

Kosode

Furisode

A wide variety of decorative processes are used in the making of kimonos, from different weaves, to embroidery, to sophisticated dyeing techniques. A few of the techniques used on the kimonos shown in this book are described below.

Shibori: a form of resist dyeing in which portions of the fabric are tied or stitched to protect it from the dye. There are many different types of *shibori*.

Kanoko: literally "deer spot"; a type of *shibori* that produces a small undyed dot on the surface of the fabric.

Kata kanoko: a method of using a stencil to produce the distinctive spot pattern of *kanoko*.

Chayazome: an early paste-resist dyeing method featuring indigo.

Yûzen: A sophisticated resist dyeing method in which the resist is hand painted or stenciled onto the fabric. When the garment was then dyed, the areas protected by the resist remained undyed. *Yûzen* is extremely flexible, allowing the artist to produce very "painterly" designs.

There are many different types of kimonos, differentiated by style or purpose. Below are the ones shown in this volume.

Kosode: The most common form of the kimono and the generic term used to describe all full-length garments.

Furisode: A kimono with long, swinging sleeves.

Katabira: An unlined summer kimono of hemp or ramie.

Awase: a lined kimono used in cooler weather.

Uchikake: an unbelted robe worn over a kosode

Katabira

The kimonos shown are taken from two portfolios published in Japan in the 1930s. Plates 1–33 are from the private collection of the late Shôjirô Nomora, a highly respected expert on Japanese costume and author of a number of books on the subject. Plates 34–60 are geisha costumes collected by the Kikyôya, a celebrated geisha house in Kyoto. The designs on the kimonos range from simple scatterings of flowers to scenes from classic literature and drama. All are unique and all are exquisite. They are presented here, not as fashion, but as art.

Awase

Uchikake

$\mathcal{K}$OSODE; fans, wisteria, peonies and other flowers enrich this embroidered and *kanoko* summer garment; c. Bunka Era [1804–1818].

小袖

𝒦OSODE; "willow-dyed" robe with embroidered birds,
leaves, and flowers; c. Bunka Era [1804–1818].

*F*URISODE; figured silk satin, embroidered with chrysanthemums and other patterns; c. Bunka Era [1804–1818].

帷子

𝒦ATABIRA; embroidered and *kata kanoko* grasses and flowers of four seasons interspersed with diaper patterns; c. Bunka Era [1804–1818].

K ATABIRA; this loose weave kimono is decorated with peonies and waterfalls from
hem to under the shoulders in a style known as *takasuso* (high hem); n. d.

振袖

$\mathcal{F}$URISODE; *kata kanoko* and embroidered flowers of spring and autumn; c. Bunka Era [1804–1818].

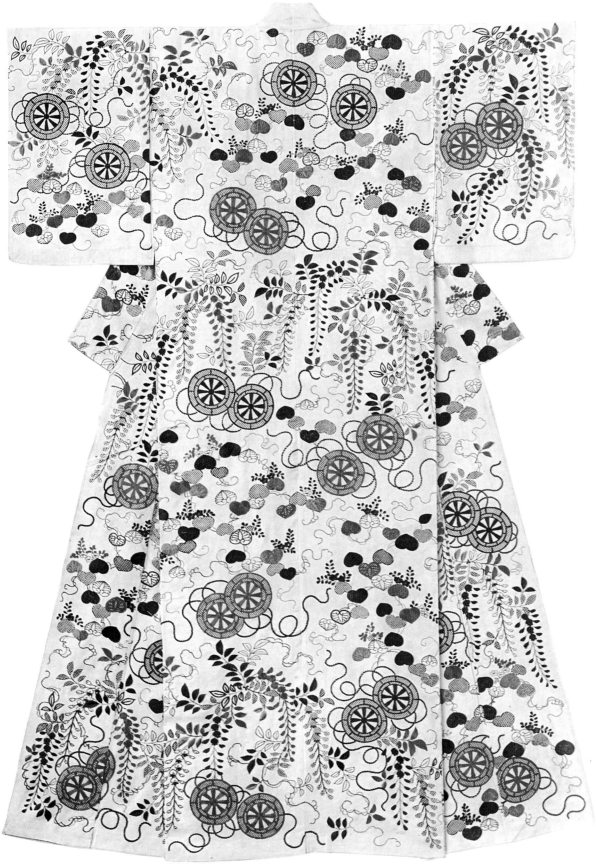

AWASE; *kata kanoko* and embroidered motifs of the aoi plant, wheels, and wisteria are featured on this robe; c. Bunsei Era [1818–1830].

𝒜 WASE; petals from the cherry blossoms at the top of this *yûzen* and embroidered robe fall amidst rain, while peonies, iris, and other flowers grow alongside a stream at the bottom; c. Bunka Era [1804–1818].

𝒦ATABIRA; maple leaf crests are embroidered on the shoulders and sleeves, while a *yûzen* and embroidered chrysanthemum pattern is featured at the hem; c. Bunsei Era [1818–1830].

𝒦OSODE; crepe-weave robe with embroidered trees and spring flowers; c. Kaei Era [1848–1854].

*K*ATABIRA; this embroidered garment features early fall flowers growing alongside a flowing stream; c. Bunsei Era [1818–1830].

帷子

𝒦ATABIRA; embroidered red-and-white morning glories bloom at
the hem of this summer robe; c. Bunsei Era [1818–1830].

𝒦 OSODE; embroidered leaves and flowers are scattered on a bold woven arrow pattern; c. Kaei Era [1848–1854].

帷子

𝒦ATABIRA; summer robe with embroidered flowers
at the top and hem; c. Ansei Era [1854–1860].

振
袖

ℱURISODE; this garment is richly embroidered with motifs from various Noh plays—a
stream, waterfalls, a lion, a decorated cart, and, from top to bottom, flowers and
trees of winter, fall, summer, and spring; c. Bunka Era [1804–1818].

帷子

Ｋatabira; the elaborate *kata kanoko* and embroidered "high hem" design includes streams, plank bridges, houses, monkeys, trees, and blossoms; c. Bunka Era [1804–1818].

振袖

FURISODE; *kata kanoko* and embroidered "high hem" design of waterfalls and blossoms; c. Bunka Era [1804–1818].

𝒦OSODE; this *yûzen* and embroidered robe features decorated carts among streams, snow-covered trees, and flowers; c. Bunka Era [1804–1818].

小袖

KOSODE; *yûzen* and embroidered pattern of flowers and *tatami* mats at the hem with embroidered crests at the top; c. Kansei Era [1789–1801].

帷子

*K*ATABIRA; crepe weave decorated with *chayazome* and
embroidered patterns; c. Bunka Era [1804–1818].

𝒦ATABIRA; *chayazome* and embroidered design of feathers, storm clouds, and streams from the hem to below the shoulders; c. Kansei Era [1789–1801].

小袖

$\mathcal{K}$OSODE; *yûzen* and embroidered "high hem" design of swallows and wisteria; c. Bunsei Era [1818–1830].

振袖

ℱURISODE; houses, fences, boats, snow-covered trees and flowers, and a horse
fill an elaborate embroidered winter landscape; c. Bunka Era [1804–1818].

打
掛

𝒰CHIKAKE; embroidered design of pine and aoi plants
and a golden lion; c. Tenmei Era [1781–1789].

振
袖

*F*URISODE; hawks soar above a winter landscape on this *yûzen* and embroidered robe; c. Bunka Era [1804–1818].

AWASE; crepe weave robe, patterned with *yûzen* and embroidered designs; c. Bunka Era [1804–1818].

$\mathcal{K}$OSODE; *yūzen* and embroidered *yatsuhasi* (a chapter in *The Tales of Ise*) design of iris, plank bridges, and a marsh; c. Bunka Era [1804–1818].

小袖

KOSODE; *kata kanoko* and embroidered motifs taken from
Ashikari, a Noh play; c. Bunka Era [1804–1818].

振袖

$\mathcal{F}$URISODE; "high hem" embroidered design of flowers, trees, plank bridges, and ribbons; c. Bunka Era [1804–1818].

振袖

*F*URISODE; "high hem" embroidered design featuring Genji carts paired with a straw hat,
a reference to Nara-period poetess Ono no Komachi; c. Bunka Era [1804–1818].

𝒦OSODE; *yûzen* and embroidered flowers fill the area from hem to waist, while calligraphy is embroidered across the top; c. Tenmei Era [1781–1789].

振
袖

$\mathcal{F}$URISODE; this robe features a *chayazome* pattern of iris
from hem to waist; c. Kansei Era [1789–1801].

𝒦ATABIRA; the *yûzen* and embroidered "high hem" design features
motifs taken from a medieval tale; c. Bunsei Era [1818–1830].

小袖

_K_osode; the lower portion features an elaborate embroidered marsh landscape; while plum blossoms cover the sleeves and shoulders; c. Bunka Era [1804–1818].

*K*OSODE; richly embroidered butterfly kites soar above clouds
and mountains filled with pine branches; n.d.

小袖

*K*OSODE; waterfalls were a common motif on kimonos in the Edo period;
this robe also features lions and peonies, both symbols of nobility; n.d.

$\mathcal{K}$OSODE; cranes, like those embroidered on this kimono, are considered a symbol of longevity in Japanese art; n.d.

$\mathcal{K}$OSODE; the embroidered symbols seen here, including the "purse of inexhaustible riches" at the lower right, depict the "myriad treasures" that ensure prosperity, long life, and good fortune; n.d.

𝓕URISODE; a single bird flies among bamboo and aoi
plants on this richly embroidered robe; n.d.

𝒦OSODE; the rabbit and wave motif seen on the lower portion was popular in the Momoyama and early Edo periods; above are the sails of several boats; n.d.

*F*URISODE; the sparrow is frequently paired with bamboo
grass in Japanese art as in this winter robe; n.d.

小袖

𝒦OSODE; *yamabushi* (warrior monks) decorate
the top and bottom of this kimono; n.d.

𝒦OSODE; embroidered design featuring *yamabushi*
resting in the shadow of Mount Fuji; n.d.

𝒦OSODE; monkeys play among the branches of peach trees, a reference
to Chinese tales about the fruit of immortality; n.d.

KATABIRA; wisteria, a symbol of long life, prosperity, and good
fortune, and family crests adorn this summer garment; n.d.

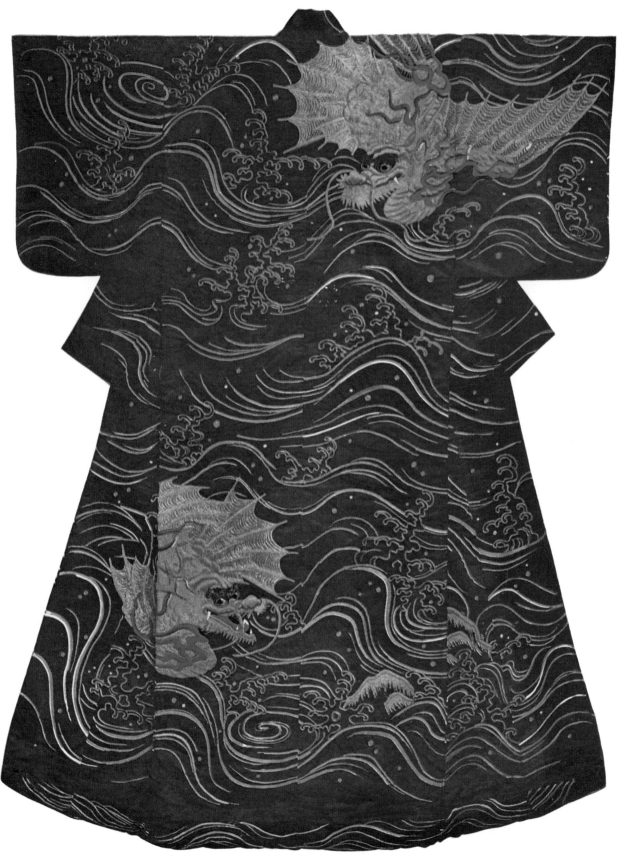

*K*OSODE; dragons, although they sometimes ascended to the heavens, were believed to live underwater. Here, finely detailed dragons, embroidered in gold thread, swim among the waves; n.d.

*F*URISODE; flowers of many seasons including peonies, iris, cherry blossoms, and chrysanthemums are embroidered on this robe; n.d.

小袖

𝒦 OSODE; two embroidered cranes fly among golden pine branches on this textured-weave kimono; n.d.

小袖

𝒦osode; a falcon, the emblem of the Japanese warrior class, soars above snow-covered pine branches on this winter garment; n. d.

小袖

𝒦OSODE; butterflies flit among chrysanthemum
blossoms on this autumn garment; n. d.

$\mathcal{K}$OSODE; pheasants, a popular theme in Japanese art,
are often paired with cherry blossoms; n. d.

小袖

𝒦OSODE; embroidered maple leaves fill the upper portion, while two human figures dominate the lower portion of this autumn landscape; n. d.

𝓕URISODE; the design at the bottom, featuring cherry blossoms and kimonos draped over a clothesline, is known as "whose sleeves," a reference to a tenth-century poem; at the top are *taiko* drums and a *torikabuto* cap, used in *bugaki*, an ancient form of music and dance; n. d.

*K*OSODE; embroidered chrysanthemums and other fall flowers
are interspersed with geometric patterns; n. d.

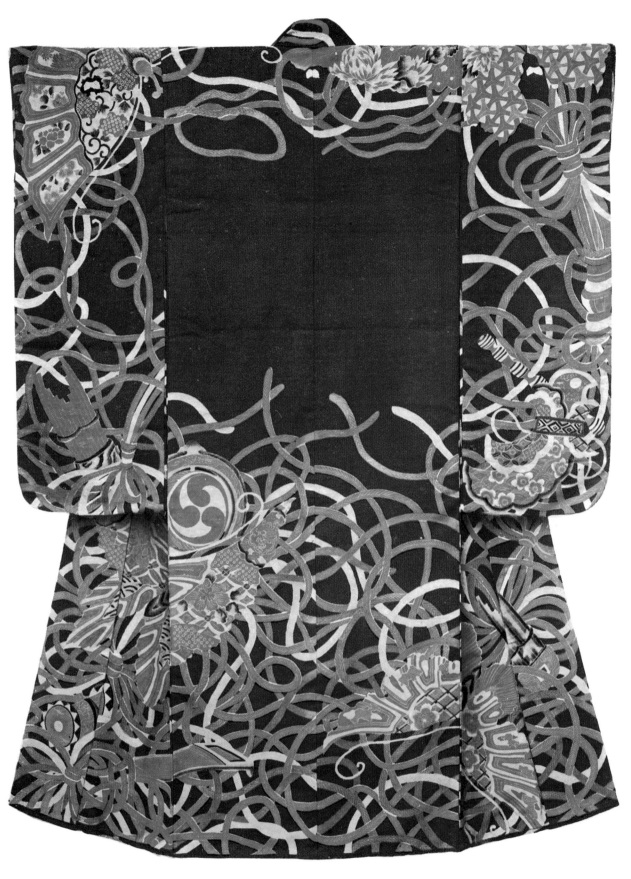

振袖

𝒻URISODE; *tarikabuto* caps, *taiko* drums, and other *bugaku*
𝒻implements are featured on this colorful robe; n.d.

振袖

FURISODE; the plover, a symbol of perseverance, is shown
with the chevrons of the blue wave motif; n. d.

ℋOSODE; wild iris combine with plank bridges to form a design known as *Yyatahashi*, alluding to the *Tales of Ise*, a Japanese literary classic; n. d.

帷子

KATABIRA; this summer garment, dyed in graduated colors
at the hem, is decorated with flowering trees; n. d.

*K*ATABIRA; human figures decorate the lower portion
of this two-colored, textured–weave robe; n. d.

帷子

K̲ATABIRA; three embroidered crests adorn the top, while the hem features
flowers, screens, baskets, and the "whose sleeves" design; n. d.